© Firefly Books

GREAT PEOPLE – GREAT FEATS (C. BK. Pg. 3)

Choose words from the cloud to fill in the boxes correctly.

AF796994

Galileo *Albert Einstein*

John Walker *Isaac Newton*

James Watt

1) He dropped objects of different weights from the Leaning Tower of Pisa.

2) The first practical matches were made in England by him.

3) He made great discoveries about gravity.

4) His theory related the gravitational field to the electric, magnetic and electromagnetic fields.

5) He watched his mother's kettle boil and invented the first steam engine.

© Firefly Books

Write a few lines on 'Japan'.

(1)____

(2)____

(3)____

(4)____

(5)____

(6)____

(7)____

(8)____

What are the things Japan has gifted to the world ? Choose from the list and write them down.

Judo *Noh Drama* *Ballet Dance*
Origami *The Ramayana* *Pyramids*
Zen *Taj Mahal* *Disneyland*

(1) ____________________ (2) ____________________

(3) ____________________ (4) ____________________

© Firefly Books

MEDIUM OF EXCHANGE (C. BK. Pg. 6)

Find the currency of each country from the cloud. Write them in the boxes provided to your right.

Euro Dirham Naira Taka Rupee
Yuan Baht Yen Rupee Dollar

1) Morocco

2) Japan

3) Nigeria

4) Portugal

5) China

6) Pakistan

7) Thailand

8) America

9) Bangladesh

10) India

© Firefly Books

Find out the names of the instruments with the help of the pictures.

(1) 

It begins with the alphabet 'G'

(2) 

It begins with the alphabet 'P'

(3) 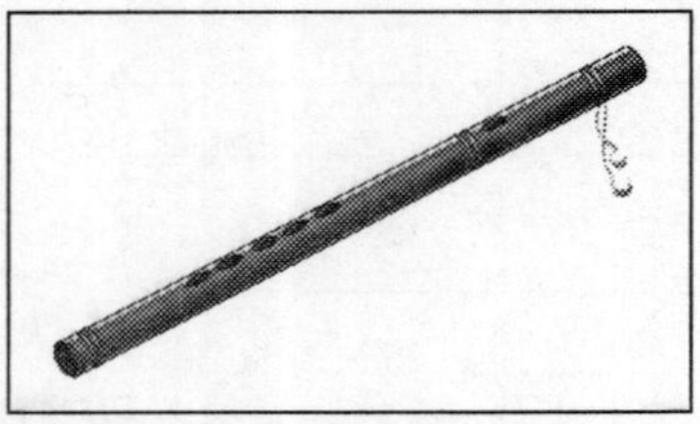

It begins with the alphabet 'F'

(4) 

It begins with the alphabet 'V'

(5) 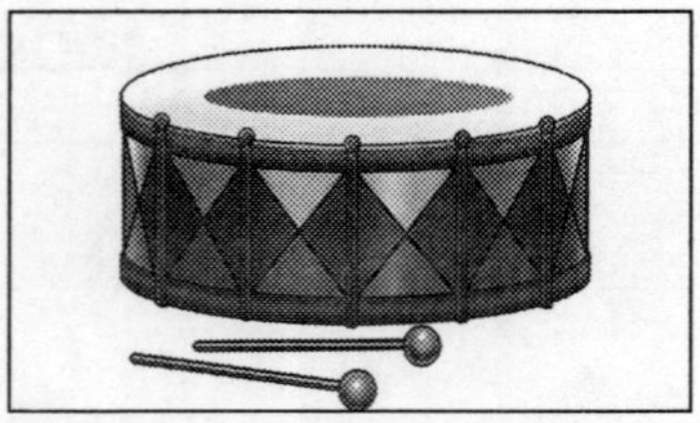

It begins with the alphabet 'D'

(6) 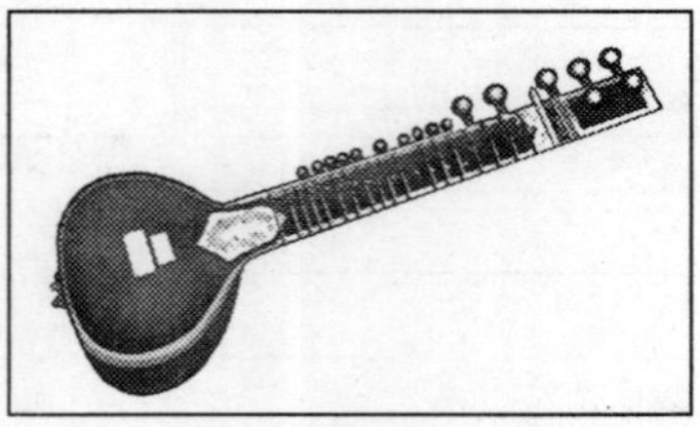

It begins with the alphabet 'S'

(7) 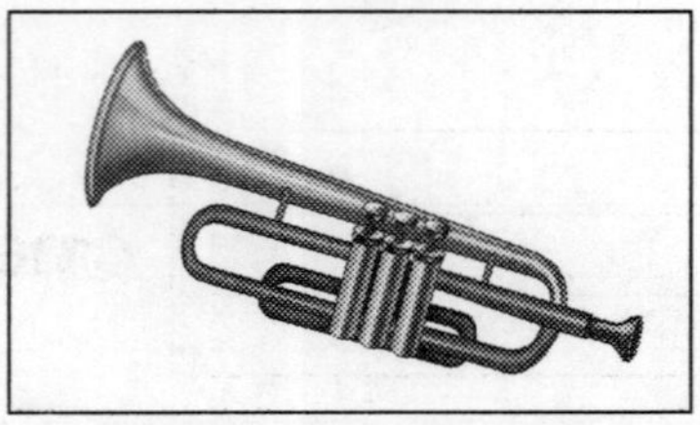

It begins with the alphabet 'T'

© Firefly Books

IMPORTANT MONUMENTS (C. BK. Pg. 8)

Find out and write down the country where these monuments are found. Begin the names of the countries with capital letters.

1) The Great Pyramid of Giza ______ pgeyt

2) The Temple of Artemis ______ eutkyr

3) The Porcelain Pagoda of Nanking ______ achin

4) The Colosseum ______ moer

5) The Golden Temple ______ niiad

6) The Statue of Liberty ______ cmeiaar

© Firefly Books

GREAT PERSONALITIES (C. BK. Pg. 9)

These are the people who changed the world. Read each description and write the person's name.

(1) A famous explorer who reached America by sailing towards the West across the Atlantic Ocean.

(2) He is one of the richest men on earth. He created the first computer programme.

(3) He was a German leader who hated Jews. He killed millions of them.

(4) He put forward the Theory of Evolution.

(5) He was the greatest playwright in the English language.

Help Box

Charles Darwin, William Shakespeare, Adolf Hitler, Bill Gates, Christopher Columbus.

© Firefly Books

FLAGS AND COUNTRIES (C. BK. Pg. 10)

Get pictures of Flags of different countries. Stick them here and write the name of the country and its currency.

Country ____________________ Country ____________________

Currency ____________________ Currency ____________________

Country ____________________ Country ____________________

Currency ____________________ Currency ____________________

Country ____________________ Country ____________________

Currency ____________________ Currency ____________________

© Firefly Books

POPULATION FACTS (C. BK. Pg. 11)

1. Given below are names of the most populous cities in the world. Arrange them in descending order (i.e. beginning with the highest population down to the lowest in the group).

Cities -

Cities	
Moscow	(1) ______________________
Mumbai	(2) ______________________
Shanghai	(3) ______________________
Tokyo	(4) ______________________
Istanbul	(5) ______________________

(Ans. Shanghai, Mumbai, Moscow, Istanbul, Tokyo).

2. Complete these blanks to get the answers :

(a) People of this country live the longest. A__d__ __r__.

(b) The fourteen unhappiest countries are all in this continent. E__ __op__

(c) The largest country in the world is __us__ __ __ __.

(d) More than 90% of people in Bhutan are engaged in ag__ __c__ __ __ __r__.

(e) This is one country which is 100% urbanised. S__ng__ __ __r__.

Help Box

Andorra, Russia, agriculture, Europe, Singapore.

© Firefly Books

LANGUAGES (C. BK. Pg. 12)

Below is a list of countries. Write the official languages of these countries in the blanks provided alongside.

(1) Netherlands - ______________________________.

(2) USA - ______________________________.

(3) Norway - ______________________________.

(4) India - ______________________________.

(5) Iran - ______________________________.

Here is a puzzle in which the words used are those English has taken from other languages. Solve the puzzle with the help of the clues given.

Clues:

1. What we have with curry.
2. A type of science.
3. A type of garment we wear.
4. A type of chocolate we like to eat.
5. A creature.
6. A precious stone.

© Firefly Books

THE SOLAR SYSTEM (C. BK. Pg. 13)

With the help of the clues given write the names of the planets in our solar system.

(1) It was named after the speedy messenger of the gods.

(2) The largest planet of the solar system.

(3) The planet we live in.

(4) The planet with rings.

(5) Some of our space probes have flown past or landed on this planet.

(6) The planet rotates backwards i.e. East to West.

© Firefly Books

ROUGH AND TOUGH (C. BK. Pg. 15)

Use the clues to name the correct type of rock.

(1) The Taj Mahal is made of this rock.

(2) These rocks are found from volcanoes

(3) This rock is used to write on blackboards.

(4) The Red Fort in Delhi is made of this rock.

(5) This rock is used in the preparation of cement.

(6) This is a rock used in electrical goods.

Help Box

Chalk, Marble, Granite, Limestone, Red Sandstone, Mica.

© Firefly Books

SPORTS (C. BK. Pg. 16)

Name the games that you see in the pictures.

______________________ ______________________ ______________________

______________________ ______________________ ______________________

? Question Time:

(1) Which game do you enjoy the most ?

____

(2) Which is your favourite sports channel ? Who is your favourite sports star ?

____

ALL ABOUT BOOKS (C. BK. Pg. 17)

hoose answers from the bracket given below and fill in the blanks.

dictionary atlas
directory biography
autobiography thesaurus

A book about someone's life written by another person

A book with an alphabetical list of words and their meanings

A book of maps

A book with alphabetical lists of names and addresses of people and organizations

A book organized to show words with similar meanings

A book about a person's life written by the person himself

© Firefly Books

GAMES YOU PLAY (C. BK. Pg. 18)

Name the games that you see in the pictures given below.

(1)

(2)

(3)

(4)

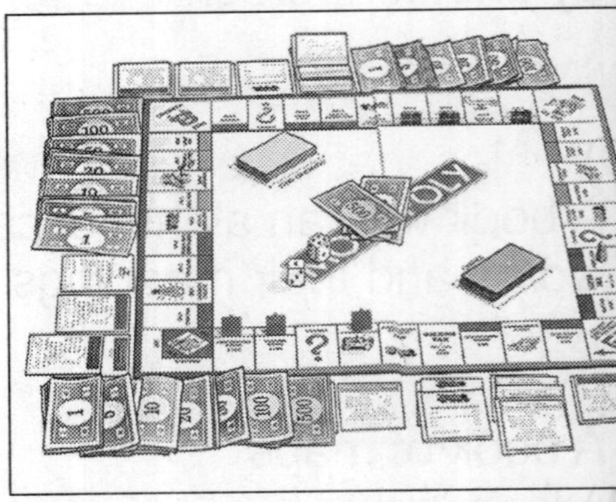

(5)

(6)

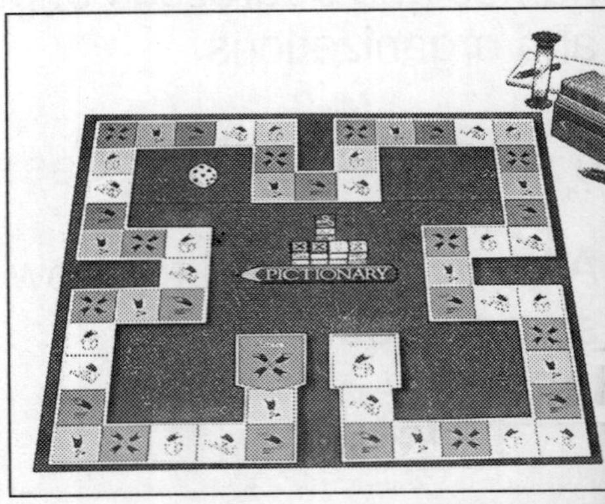

SAILING VESSELS (C. BK. Pg. 20)

ind the answers with the help of the description given and write he answers in the space provided.

1) A boat with two hulls side by side is called

2) A sailing or engine-powered ship used for pleasure is called a

3) Ships that go under water are known as

4) A Ship that carries oil from oil fields to refineries is called a

5) A ship that takes passengers and vehicles from one port to another is known as

Help Box

Oil Tanker, Merchant Ship, Catamaran, Cruise liner, Submarines.

© Firefly Books

ELECTRONIC GADGETS (C. BK. Pg. 21)

Here are a few electronic gadgets. Find out the work they do and fil in the blanks.

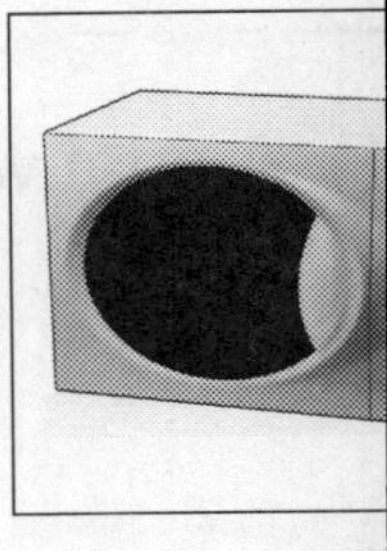

A microwave is used for ______________________.

(washing, heating, cooling)

A refrigerator works on ______________________.

(electricity, petrol, diesel)

A vacuum cleaner cleans by sucking in ______________________.

(smoke, dust, solids)

An air-conditioner keeps the temperature ______________________

(cool, hot, humid)

A mixer is a gadget used for ______________________.

(grinding, cooking, washing)

A generator is used for generating ______________________.

(water, electricity, oil)

LUXURY TRANSPORT (C. BK. Pg. 22)

Get pictures of different models of cars from newspapers or magazines. Stick them here and write their names.

© Firefly Books

NATURAL POWER RESOURCES (C. BK. Pg. 23)

Match the description in column 'A' with the words in column 'B'. Than write your answers in the blanks provided at the bottom.

'A'	'B'
(1) It is naturally formed beneath the earth. It is collected in pipes and sent to various places.	(a) Coal
(2) It is a form of energy that is produced with the help of the wind.	(b) Hydropower
(3) It is a source of energy and is made from plants that lived and died years ago.	(c) Solar Energy
(4) The sun's warmth can be stored to produce electricity.	(d) Wind Energy
(5) Flowing water produces electricity. This is an important power source.	(e) Natural Gas

Answers (1) ______ (2) ______

(3) ______ (4) ______ (5) ______

WATER IS LIFE (C. BK. Pg. 24)

Answer the following questions about water by filing in the blanks. Take help from the Help Box.

1) We cannot drink sea water because it is

2) The best way we can save water in the house is by saving water while

3) The biggest source of water to us is the

4) Water exists in the form of matter.

5) The largest river in India is

6) Animals which live on land as well as water are called as

7) The biggest river in the world

8) Places with very scanty rainfall may turn into

Help Box

Nile, salty, liquid, rain, Ganga, amphibians, bathing, deserts.

© Firefly Books

BODY ORGANS AND THEIR FUNCTIONS (C. BK. Pg. 25)

Observe the pictures. Write the names of the body parts against them. Put a sign '✓' in the boxes for the work they do.

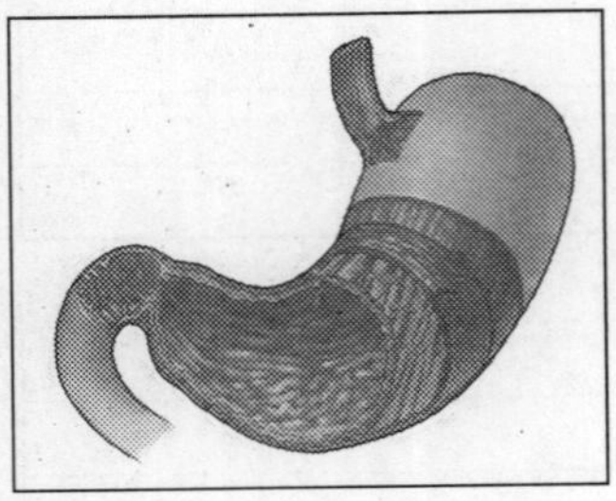

__________ (1) Produces gastric juice ☐

(2) Throws out waste material ☐

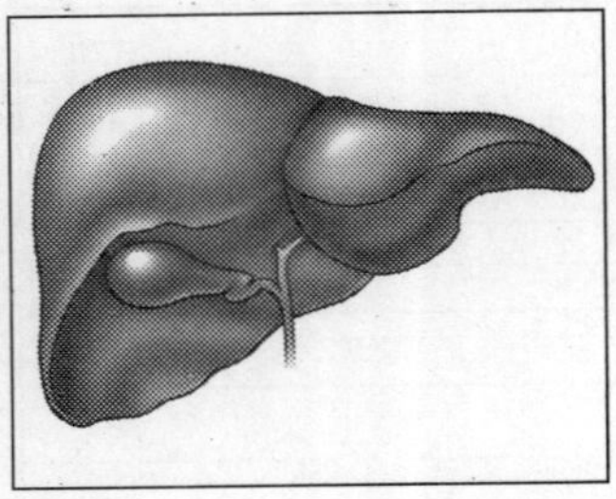

__________ (1) Produces saliva ☐

(2) Produces bile ☐

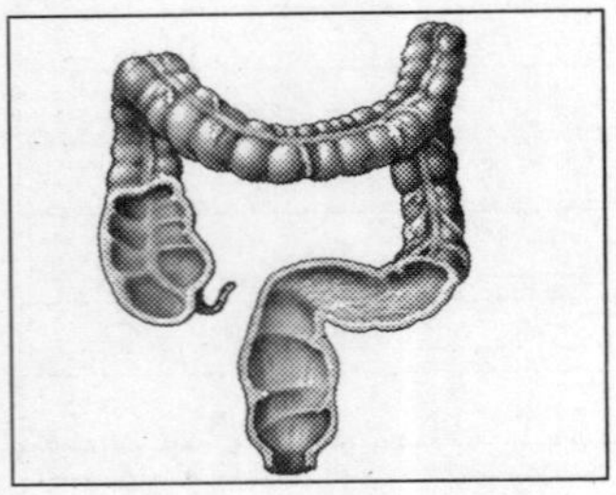

__________ (1) Absorbs food ☐

(2) Takes in air ☐

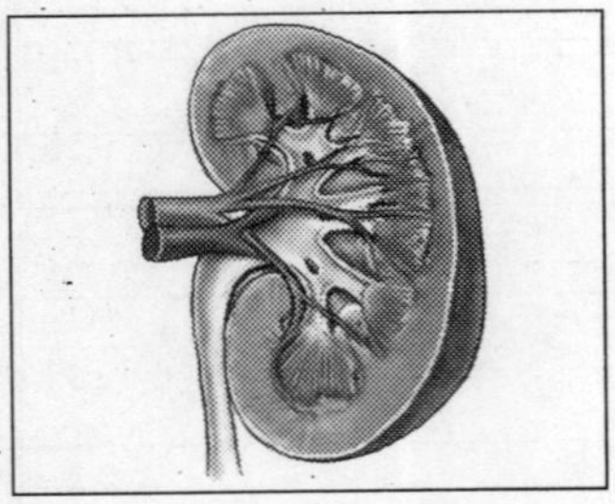

__________ (1) Throws out waste matter ☐

(2) Absorbs food ☐

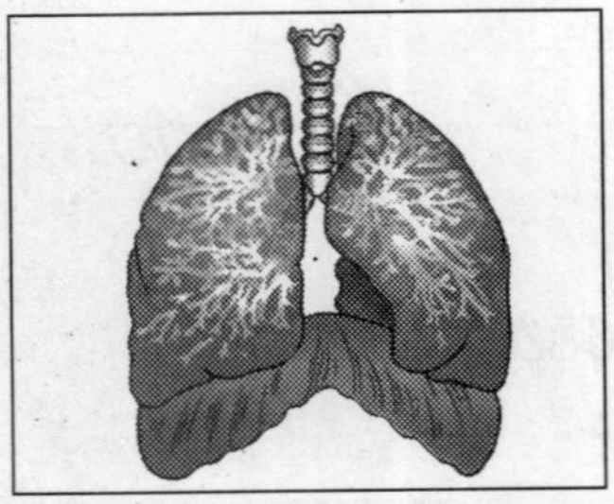

__________ (1) Gives out saliva ☐

(2) Takes in oxygen ☐

FOODS AND THEIR NUTRIENTS (*C. BK. Pg.* 26)

Name the following (you can take help of your parents or teachers).

(1) 3 food items rich in Fats.

(a) (b) (c)

(2) 3 food items rich in Protein.

(a) (b) (c)

(3) 3 food items rich in Vitamins.

(a) (b) (c)

(4) 3 food items rich in Iron.

(a) (b) (c)

(5) 3 food items rich in Carbohydrates.

(a) (b) (c)

© Firefly Books

Answer these questions about snakes :

(1) Snakes are a

(a) *Kind of lizard* (b) *amphibian* (c) *reptile*

(2) The largest snake is

(a) *Boa constrictor* (b) *Anaconda* (c) *Python*

(3) A particular characteristic of snakes is that they are

(a) *cylindrical* (b) *shiny* (c) *fat*

(4) The largest poisonous snake in the world is the

(a) *Anaconda* (b) *King Cobra* (c) *Rattle Sna*

(5) Which is the largest snake in the world ?

(a) *Anaconda* (b) *Python* (c) *King Cobr*

[**Ans.:** (1-c), (2-b), (3-b), (4-b), (5-b)]

KNOWING ABOUT BIRDS (C. BK. Pg. 30)

Choose words from the cloud to fill in the boxes correctly.

Penguins *Swallows*

Pelican *Ostrich* *Nightingale*

1) A bird that sings sweetly

2) The fastest running bird in the world

3) Migrating birds that move from England to South Africa

4) These birds are found in ice-bound regions, near water bodies that are frozen.

5) A goose-like water bird which has a

© Firefly Books

ANIMALS AND THEIR IDENTITY (C. BK. Pg. 31)

Here is some information. Use them to fill in the boxes.

(1) He is called 'the king of the jungle'.

(2) He has a long neck and eats leaves from trees. He has spots on his body.

(3) He has a long trunk and a huge body.

(4) Man evolved from this animal. It took millions of years to be what he is today.

(5) He is the enemy of the Tiger. He ejects his quills at other animals when he is angry.